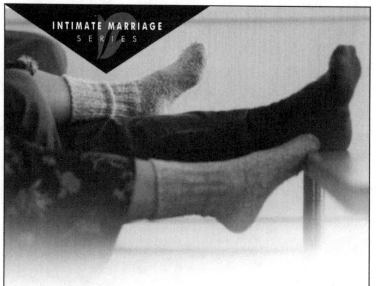

INTIMATE MARRIAGE
SERIES

COMMUNICATION

Dan B. Allender
and Tremper Longman III

6 STUDIES FOR INDIVIDUALS, COUPLES OR GROUPS

InterVarsity Press
Downers Grove, Illinois

InterVarsity Press
P.O. Box 1400, Downers Grove, IL 60515-1426
World Wide Web: www.ivpress.com
E-mail: mail@ivpress.com

InterVarsity Press® is the book-publishing division of InterVarsity Christian Fellowship/USA®, a student movement active on campus at hundreds of universities, colleges and schools of nursing in the United States of America, and a member movement of the International Fellowship of Evangelical Students. For information about local and regional activities, write Public Relations Dept., InterVarsity Christian Fellowship/USA, 6400 Schroeder Rd., P.O. Box 7895, Madison, WI 53707-7895, or visit the IVCF website at <www.intervarsity.org>.

Unless otherwise indicated, all Scripture quotations are taken from the Holy Bible, New Living Translation, copyright ©1996, 2004. Used by permission of Tyndale House Publishers, Inc., Wheaton, Illinois 60189. All rights reserved.

Design: Cindy Kiple

Images: Ryan McVay/Getty Images

ISBN 0-8308-2136-8

Printed in the United States of America ∞

P	18	17	16	15	14	13	12	11	10	9	8	7	6	5	4	3	2	1
Y	18	17	16	15	14	13	12	11	10	09	08	07	06	05				

CONTENTS

Welcome to Intimate Marriage Bible Studies 5

1 THE POWER OF WORDS 9
Genesis 1:1-8; selections from Proverbs

2 TALK THAT HURTS RELATIONSHIPS 15
Selections from Proverbs

3 TALK THAT BUILDS RELATIONSHIPS 21
Selections from Proverbs

4 A TIME TO BE QUIET AND A TIME TO SPEAK UP 27
Ecclesiastes 3:1-7; selections from Proverbs

5 THE ART OF LISTENING AND REFLECTION 33
Selections from Proverbs

6 THE COUPLE THAT PRAYS TOGETHER 40
1 Corinthians 7:3-6; Romans 8:22-23, 26-27

Study Notes 46

113659

WELCOME TO
INTIMATE MARRIAGE
BIBLE STUDIES

COMMUNICATION

Among all of God's creatures, human beings have the most highly developed ability to communicate with one another. We can use physical gestures, write letters, and send e-mails and instant messages to communicate, but nothing is more intimate than talking. Through talking to others we both reveal ourselves and learn about another person. Through such knowledge a relationship grows.

How absolutely critical to a marriage, the most intimate of human relationships, that a husband and wife talk to one another! But it is not just any kind of talk. Indeed too much or foolish talk will break down a marriage as sure as anything. We need to reflect on how we talk to each other.

But talking is just one part of communication. We must also learn the art of good listening. Nothing is more aggravating than a friend or relative who hogs the conversation. A good marriage is characterized by wise listening as well as wise speech.

The following Bible studies utilize relevant passages from Scripture to help us think through what makes for good communication in marriage. Improved communication results in stronger marriages.

TAKING MARRIAGE SERIOUSLY

Most of us want to have a good marriage. Those who don't have a good relationship yearn for a better one, and those who have a good one want even more intimacy.

We want to know our spouse and be known by them. We want to be loved and to love. In short, we want the type of marriage desired by God from the beginning when he created the institution of marriage and defined it as involving leaving parents, weaving a life of intimacy together and cleaving in sexual bliss.

These studies delve into the wisdom of the Bible in order to learn what it takes to have not just a "good" marriage but one that enjoys the relational richness that God intended for a husband and a wife. This divinely instituted type of marriage is one that will

- Bring a husband and wife closer together
- Understand that marriage is one's primary loyalty to other human beings
- Be characterized by a growing love and knowledge of one another
- Be an arena of spiritual growth
- Allow for the healthy exposure of sin through the offer of forgiveness
- Be a crucible for showing grace
- Reflect God's love for his people
- Enjoy God's gift of sexual intimacy
- Share life's joys and troubles

- Have a part in transforming us from sinners to saints
- Bring out each other's glory as divine image bearers

And so much more! The Bible provides a wealth of insight, and these studies hope to tap its riches and bring them to bear on our marriage relationships.

USING THE STUDIES

These studies can be used in a variety of contexts—individual devotional life, by a couple together or by a small group—or in a combination of these settings. Each study includes the following components.

Open. Several quotes at the beginning give a sense of what married people say about the topic at hand. These are followed by a question that can be used for discussion. If you are using the DVD, you may want to skip this and go straight to the opening clip.

DVD Reflection. For each session we have an opening thought from Dan Allender, at times accompanied by an excerpt from our interviews with married couples to get you thinking about the topic at hand. This material will provide fresh and engaging openers for a small group as well as interesting discussion points for couples studying together. You will find a question here to discuss after you watch the DVD clip.

Study. One or more key Bible texts are included in the guide for convenience. We have chosen the New Living Translation, but you may use any version of Scripture you like. The questions in this section will take you through the key aspects of the passage and help you apply them to your marriage. Sprinkled throughout the study, you will also find commentary to enrich your experience.

For the Couple. Here's an opportunity to make an application and commitment, which is specific to your marriage.

Bonus. These are further ideas for study on your own. Or if you are studying with a group, take time to do the bonus item with your spouse during the week.

We hope that these studies enrich your marriage. We encourage you to be brutally honest with yourself and tactfully honest with your spouse. If you are willing to be honest with yourself and with the Scripture, then God will do great things for your marriage. That is our prayer.

THE POWER OF WORDS

"Sticks and stones may break my bones, but words will never hurt me."

▶ OPEN

The popular "sticks and stones" saying is memorable, but it's not true. All of us have experienced the pain of harmful words. How does negative communication affect a marriage?

▶ DVD REFLECTION

How have words made a lasting impression on you?

▶ STUDY

Read Genesis 1:1-8.

In the beginning God created the heavens and the earth. ²The earth was formless and empty, and darkness covered the deep waters. And the Spirit of God was hovering over the surface of the waters.

³Then God said, "Let there be light," and there was light. ⁴And

God saw that the light was good. Then he separated the light from the darkness. [5]God called the light "day" and the darkness "night."

And evening passed and morning came, marking the first day.

[6]Then God said, "Let there be a space between the waters, to separate the waters of the heavens from the waters of the earth." [7]And that is what happened. God made this space to separate the waters of the earth from the waters of the heavens. [8]God called the space "sky."

And evening passed and morning came, marking the second day.

1. In Genesis, God speaks at the time of creation. What effect does the divine speech have?

CONTEXT: GENESIS 1

Genesis 1 famously announces that God created the universe and that as a result everything is dependent on him for existence. Over a period of six days God brings forth the world, and he rests on the seventh day. Thus creation is presented as the work of a divine sculptor. In the first three days, God creates the realms of light and darkness, water and sky, and finally land, and in the second three days he fills each of these realms in turn with the sun, moon and stars, fish and birds, and animals and human beings.

What does this tell us about the power of words?

2. Have God's words to you—perhaps in Scripture, perhaps in a "still small voice"—ever created something new in your life or changed your life's direction? If so, tell that story.

3. What implications does the power of divine speech in Genesis 1 have for our own human speech?

Read the following selections from Proverbs.

From a wise mind [heart] comes wise speech;
    the words of the wise are persuasive. (16:23)

Wise words are like deep waters;
    wisdom flows from the wise like a bubbling brook. (18:4)

The words of the godly are like sterling silver;
    the heart of a fool is worthless. (10:20)

²³Smooth words may hide a wicked heart,
    just as a pretty glaze covers a clay pot.
²⁴People may cover their hatred with pleasant words,
    but they're deceiving you.

²⁵They pretend to be kind, but don't believe them.
    their hearts are full of many evils.
²⁶While their hatred may be concealed by trickery,
    their wrongdoing will finally be exposed in public.
        (26:23-26)

The wicked are trapped by their own words,
    but the godly escape such trouble. (12:13)

The fool's proud talk becomes a rod that beats him,
    but the words of the wise keep them safe. (14:3)

Spouting off before listening to the facts
    is both shameful and foolish. (18:13)

The tongue can bring death or life;
    those who love to talk will reap the consequences. (18:21)

▼

CONTEXT: READING PROVERBS

There is no book quite like Proverbs in the rest of the Bible. The first nine chapters are long speeches by a father (or Woman Wisdom) to a son. Then in chapters 10 and following we encounter a collection of two- or three-line proverbial sayings that cover a host of topics, including wealth and poverty, laziness, family matters, and speech. Since there is no overarching structure to this section of the book, it is appropriate to take proverbs out of their literary context and reflect on them in isolation or, as here, to draw together proverbs that teach on the same or a similar theme.

4. Reread Proverbs 16:23; 18:4; 10:20. What do these proverbs say about the relationship between a person's words and that person's heart?

5. Does Proverbs 26:23-26 undermine the connection established between words and the heart in the earlier proverbs? Why or why not?

▼

THE HEBREW HEART

In English when we speak of someone's heart, we typically mean character, with emphasis on emotions. When we want to speak of a person's intelligence, we say they are "brainy." Ancient Hebrew has some overlap with but also difference from modern English usage. In Hebrew heart also points to one's character or core personality, but any emphasis is on intelligence rather than emotion. This is why the Hebrew word for "heart" (leb) is sometimes translated "mind" in contemporary translations.

6. Reread Proverbs 12:13; 14:3; 18:13, 21. What does this collection of proverbs have to say about the effects of people's words?

7. As you consider all these Scriptures, what wisdom do they offer for communication in your marriage?

▶ **FOR THE COUPLE**

Reflect on how you communicate with each other. What patterns do you notice?

What are the strengths and the weaknesses of your communication pattern?

What would you like to change?

▶ **BONUS**

Read Psalm 46. What encouragement does it offer regarding the power of God's speech in the world and in your life?

2

TALK THAT HURTS RELATIONSHIPS

"She just doesn't listen to me. I come home, and she is making dinner; I tell her about my day, and it's as if she never heard me."

"I hate it when I wake up and want to talk about my worries. He always tells me to wait till later, and later never comes."

"I give him a bit of constructive criticism and he just blasts me."

"I just can't help it. I tell myself I will just drive her away. But then something compels me to criticize anyway."

▶ OPEN

Even good marriages falter from time to time in the area of communication. Sometimes we don't hear each other even if we physically hear the words. The possibilities for miscommunication are tremendous, and poor communication can completely undermine a relationship. Why don't we listen to each other?

▶ DVD REFLECTION

How would you define "junk food" talk in a marriage?

CONTEMPTUOUS SPEECH

Contempt is a feeling of revulsion and utter distaste toward something or someone. To speak to someone with contempt is to attempt to embarrass or disgrace them. The consequence of such speech is to drive them away. Contemptuous speech is mocking, scornful, extremely disrespectful. Researchers from the University of Washington have uncovered data that indicates that the number-one predictor of significant marital conflict and eventual divorce is contemptuous speech.

▶ **STUDY**

Read the following selections from Proverbs.

The godly are showered with blessings;
   the words of the wicked conceal violent intentions. (10:6)

With their words, the godless destroy their friends;
   but knowledge will rescue the righteous. (11:9)

Upright citizens are good for a city and make it prosper,
   but the talk of the wicked tears it apart. (11:11)

The words of the wicked are like a murderous ambush,
   but the words of the godly save lives. (12:6)

Some people make cutting remarks,
   but the words of the wise bring healing.
Truthful words stand the test of time,
   but lies are soon exposed. (12:18-19)

The mouths of fools are their ruin;
   they trap themselves with their lips. (18:7)

Spouting off before listening to the facts
 is both shameful and foolish. (18:13)

Throw out the mocker, and fighting goes, too;
 Quarrels and insults will disappear. (22:10)

Telling lies about others
 is as harmful as hitting them with an ax,
wounding them with a sword,
 or shooting them with a sharp arrow. (25:18)

Singing cheerful songs to a person with a heavy heart

 is like taking someone's coat in cold weather
 or pouring vinegar in a wound. (25:20)

A quarrelsome person starts fights
 as easily as hot embers light charcoal or fire lights wood.
 (26:21)

A loud and cheerful greeting early in the morning

 will be taken as a curse! (27:14)

Fools vent their anger,
 but the wise quietly hold it back. (29:11)

1. Based on these proverbs, what is the nature of foolish conversation?

2. How can "cheerful songs" (25:20) and "a pleasant greeting" (27:14) be considered foolish talk?

If possible, tell of a time in your own life when others' cheerful remarks were unhelpful.

READING ANTITHETICAL PROVERBS

Many proverbs in this study are what are technically called antithetical parallelisms: two-line proverbs that look at the same truth from opposite perspectives. This parallelism allows the poet to contrast wise behavior with foolish. The questions in this study focus on the side of the parallelism that teaches about foolish speech.

3. What are the consequences of foolish conversation?

4. Describe some patterns of foolish conversation that are easy for married partners to fall into.

5. What are the consequences of foolish conversation for a marriage?

6. What does Proverbs 29:11 recommend as a way to avoid destructive conversation?

How is this different from hiding or repressing your true feelings?

WHAT IS FOLLY IN PROVERBS?

In Proverbs, folly is the opposite of wisdom. On one level it is a very practical category. While wisdom is speech and behavior that promotes and enhances relationship, folly breaks it down. In the Bible, and in Proverbs in particular, wisdom and folly have a profound theological foundation. It is the "fear of God" that "is the beginning of wisdom" (Proverbs 1:7), while "the fool says in his heart that there is no God" (Psalm 14:1). Thus wisdom begins with a strong relationship with God.

▶ FOR THE COUPLE

Reflect on your own pattern of foolish speech in your marriage. Talk about areas and conversational strategies that you realize are harmful or counterproductive. How can you help each other avoid harmful talk?

Pray together for God's help to break the habit of bad conversational patterns.

Do you have time to talk with one another?

If not, what can you do to find that essential time?

▶ BONUS

Was there much teasing in your family of origin?

If teasing was common, give a couple of examples.

Was it helpful for bringing you close together, or was it harmful? Why?

What are some wise and foolish ways that humor can be used in communication between spouses?

3

TALK THAT BUILDS RELATIONSHIPS

"Just hearing his voice makes me feel so much better!"

"She knows how to say the right thing at the right time to lift my spirits."

"I know I'm not perfect, so I am glad someone feels comfortable enough to point out my weaknesses; otherwise how could I improve? And she knows how to criticize without tearing me down."

▶ OPEN

Words hurt and words heal. This study explores the healing possibility in communication. The way we speak to each other can encourage, uplift, motivate, sustain—especially within marriage. How can we speak in a way that strengthens and enriches marriage?

▶ DVD REFLECTION

What is the best thing you have learned or the best advice you have been given about communicating in a marriage?

▶ STUDY

Read the following selections from Proverbs.

People who accept discipline are on the pathway to life,
  but those who ignore correction will go astray. (10:17)

A fool's proud talk becomes a rod that beats him,
  but the words of the wise keep them safe. (14:3)

A gentle answer deflects anger,
  but harsh words make tempers flare. (15:1)

Gentle words are a tree of life;
  a deceitful tongue crushes the spirit. (15:4)

Everyone enjoys a fitting reply;
  it is wonderful to say the right thing at the right time! (15:23)

Kind words are like honey—
  sweet to the soul and healthy for the body. (16:24)

Wise words are like deep waters;
  wisdom flows from the wise like a bubbling brook. (18:4)

To one who listens, valid criticism
  is like a gold earring or other gold jewelry. (25:12)

⁴Don't answer the foolish arguments of fools,
  or you will become as foolish as they are.
⁵Be sure to answer the foolish arguments of fools,
  or they will become wise in their own estimation. (26:4-5)

Smooth words may hide a wicked heart,
  just as a pretty glaze covers a clay pot. (26:23)

An open rebuke
is better than hidden love! (27:5)

1. What insight do Proverbs 15:23 and 26:4-5 give us on healthy
   communication?

CONTRADICTORY PROVERBS?

If we are honest, it sometimes seems as if proverbs contradict each other. A good example comes from Proverbs 26:4-5, where one tells the reader to answer a fool and another not to. Which is it? It depends on the time and circumstance. We must know the person we are talking to and whether silence or conversation is going to be helpful or not. We must read the circumstance as well as the proverb to know if it applies.

This is a feature of proverbs, no matter what language they are written in. When my grandmother wanted to cook the family Thanksgiving turkey her way, she would greet my well-intentioned mother and aunt's desire to help with, "Too many cooks spoil the broth." But when she had a pile of dishes to do, she would announce, "Many hands make light work." Both are true—when spoken at the right moment.

2. How can you tell when it is the right time to say something to
   your spouse?

3. According to Proverbs 10:17; 14:3; 25:12; 27:5, how does pride
   disrupt communication?

   Why is it important, even necessary, to listen to criticism?

4. Do these proverbs give insight regarding the way we should
   criticize each other?

5. In what way are kind works like honey (16:24)?

6. Are kind words always positive and gentle?

Can criticism be kind?

7. What does Proverbs 26:23 tell us about communication skills?

▶ FOR THE COUPLE

Reflect on the way your spouse's words have encouraged, restored and helped you. Share examples with each other.

▶ BONUS

Ephesians 4:28 says, "Don't use foul and abusive language. Let everything you say be good and helpful, so that your words will be an encouragement to those who hear them." Talk with your spouse about the health of your communication. It may be wise to reflect on these categories:

• How well do we speak in the middle of a fight?

• How well do we handle talking when one of us clams up?

- Can we move from details to depth? Or do we stay in the realm of practicality without being able to talk deeply?

- Can we freely talk about our past, or are there issues that are off limits?

- Are we able to dream together and share desires?

- When one of us is stuck in a present problem, does the other quickly offer solutions? Or does he or she seek to explore feelings, desires and goals?

- Are we able to hear what the other is saying "between the lines," paying attention to each other's nonverbal communication?

A TIME TO BE QUIET AND A TIME TO SPEAK UP

"He never talks to me. I just cannot connect with him since he is sooo quiet."

"I don't think she leaves a thought unspoken. It is hard for me to pick out what's important from the ongoing deluge of words."

"Once we set apart a time each day to sit down and talk, our relationship got much, much better. It seemed to improve everything, including our sex life."

▶ OPEN

Many problems are created by a lack of self-control. Some eat too much and grow fat; some eat too little and make themselves seriously ill. Some spend too much and are soon poor; others spend too little and become miserly. Self-control is also a significant issue with speaking. How does self-control relate to our communication?

▶ DVD REFLECTION

What do you do if one of you wants to talk and the other doesn't?

WORDS AND GENDER

While it is important to avoid careless gender stereotyping, research-ers have empirically noted a difference between the genders when it comes to speech patterns. There are certainly quiet women and talkative men, but on the average, women talk more than men. In-deed, as an average a woman speaks 20,000 words a day and a man 5,000. This can lead to problems in expectation. Think of a woman with young children who has been home all day while her husband has exhausted his quota of words at work: he comes home ready to relax in silence, while his wife is ready to debrief.

▶ STUDY

Read Ecclesiastes 3:1-7.

[1]For everything there is a season,
    a time for every activity under heaven.
[2]A time to be born and a time to die.
    A time to plant and a time to harvest.
[3]A time to kill and a time to heal.
    A time to tear down and a time to build up.
[4]A time to cry and a time to laugh.
    A time to grieve and a time to dance.
[5]A time to scatter stones and a time to gather stones.
    A time to embrace and a time to turn away.
[6]A time to search and a time to quit searching.
    A time to keep and a time to throw away.

⁷A time to tear and a time to mend.

A time to be quiet and a time to speak.

Read the following selections from Proverbs.

It is foolish to belittle one's neighbor;

a sensible person keeps quiet. (11:12)

Those who control their tongue will have a long life;

opening your mouth can ruin everything. (13:3)

A truly wise person uses few words;

a person with understanding is even-tempered.

Even fools are thought wise when they keep silent;

with their mouths shut, they seem intelligent.

(17:27-28)

A fool is quick-tempered,

but a wise person stays calm when insulted. (12:16)

Better to be patient than powerful;

better to have self-control than to conquer a city. (16:32)

A person without self-control

is like a city with broken-down walls. (25:28)

Fools vent their anger,

but the wise quietly hold it back. (29:11)

1. Ecclesiastes states that there is a time to speak. What happens
   to a marriage relationship when either the husband or wife, or
   both, don't speak enough to each other?

2. What factors keep married people from talking to each other?

3. How can the factors that discourage healthy communication be overcome?

4. Ecclesiastes also states that there is a time to be quiet. What happens to a marriage relationship when either the husband or

EMOTIONAL INTELLIGENCE AND COMMUNICATION

Someone who is emotionally intelligent or mature knows when and how to express their emotions in a way that is helpful, not harmful. In a very informative book, Daniel Goleman (Emotional Intelligence [New York: Bantam, 1995]) defines emotional intelligence as "self-control, zeal and persistence and the ability to motivate oneself" (p. xii). The person who is emotionally intelligent has "abilities such as being able to motivate oneself and persist in the face of frustration; to control impulse and delay gratification; to regulate one's moods and keep distress from swamping the ability to think; to empathize and to hope" (p. 34). Goleman's concept of emotional intelligence sounds very much like the biblical idea of wisdom, and he helpfully demonstrates how these qualities have a higher correlation with success in life, including forming and maintaining healthy relationships, than I.Q.

wife, or both, speak too much to each other? (A number of the proverbs may prove helpful here.)

5. What makes self-control in speech so difficult?

6. How can we learn self-control?

7. While both speaking too much and too little are problems in many marriages, why do you think the Bible says much more about speaking too much?

▶ **FOR THE COUPLE**

Do your speech needs and patterns match the gender differences uncovered by researchers?

What other factors are at play—introverted versus extroverted personality, family-of-origin experiences, daily rhythms?

Talk together about how you can honor each other's needs and preferences.

DMZS

A demilitarized zone is a no-man's-land between two warring nations or persons. It is dangerous terrain, a boundary that one crosses at great risk. Many marriages are littered with DMZs. A DMZ comes to exist when a topic has repeatedly led to hurt, anger and withdrawal. Over time the couple learns that if they want peace, this topic must be avoided. The result is a fragile, conditional "peace when there is no peace" (Jeremiah 6:14; 8:11). This creates insecurity and hopelessness.

The only way to address a DMZ is to name the subjects of unresolved hostility and assess how to step slowly and prayerfully into each topic without blame or withdrawal. It will require concentrated prayer. It will usually mean agreeing to disagree, but making a commitment to hear the other, respect his or her views, and own the log in one's eye. Many incursions into that territory with repeated success will be required before the fear of walking in the zone is mitigated.

▶ BONUS

When reading the book of James, one cannot help but see many themes that overlap with the book of Proverbs. That is why James is often called the New Testament's wisdom book. Among these themes is a concern about the tongue. Though James's teaching is specifically directed toward those who teach in the church, it has ramifications for other relationships, including marriage.

Read James 3. How does James reinforce and further the lessons of the books of Ecclesiastes and Proverbs?

THE ART OF LISTENING AND REFLECTION

"I could talk till I'm blue in the face, but she just does not listen."

"The whole time he is talking to me, he is looking around. He hears my words and understands them, but I know he's also thinking about other things happening around him. It's almost like he is looking for someone better to talk to."

"He talks and talks. I have to interrupt to get a word in. I think he likes the sound of his own voice and couldn't care less about my opinion."

▶ OPEN

Conversation is a two-way street. It's not just a matter of talking; it also involves listening, and few of us are good listeners. We need to hear our spouse and reflect on what she or he says, but we are readily distracted. There is no easier way to offend a spouse than by not paying attention to his or her words. How has listening helped your marriage?

▶ DVD REFLECTION

What is the cost of not listening in a marriage?

▶ STUDY

Listening involves focused attention and takes discipline and practice. What does the Bible tell us about the value of good listening and the consequences of not paying attention?

Read the following selections from Proverbs.

To learn, you must love discipline;
    it is stupid to hate correction. (12:1)

Fools think their own way is right,
    but the wise listen to others. (12:15)

Pride leads to conflict;
    those who take advice are wise. (13:10)

If you ignore criticism, you will end up in poverty and
        disgrace;
    if you accept criticism, you will be honored. (13:18)

If you listen to constructive criticism,
    you will be at home among the wise.
If you reject discipline, you only harm yourself;
    but if you listen to correction, you will grow in
        understanding. (15:31-32)

Fools have no interest in understanding;
    they only want to air their own opinions. (18:2)

Intelligent people are always ready to learn.
    Their ears are open for knowledge. (18:15)

To one who listens, valid criticism
    is like a gold earring or other gold jewelry. (25:12)

An open rebuke is better
  than hidden love!
Wounds from a sincere friend
  are better than many kisses from an enemy. (27:5-6)

The heart of the godly thinks carefully before speaking;
  the mouth of the wicked overflows with evil words. (15:28)

Plans succeed through good counsel;
  don't go to war without wise advice. (20:18)

There is more hope for a fool
  than for one who speaks without thinking. (29:20)

▼

PROVERBS AND MARRIAGE

The proverbs we consider in this study are not specifically for married couples. They can enrich and guide all kinds of relationships. However, they may be applied to marriage; for the purpose of this study, we recommend that they be read with marriage specifically in mind.

1. What is the foolish behavior described in Proverbs 18:2?

How might this behavior manifest itself in a marriage?

THE FOOL

Proverbs states its truths in a very matter-of-fact, black-and-white manner. There are the wise, and there are fools. Calling someone a fool seems strong language to us, and we certainly don't like to think of ourselves as fools. The true fool is one who rejects God (Psalm 14:1; Proverbs 1:7). However, even godly people can resemble fools when they behave in certain ways. The proverbs point out foolish behaviors to get those who are really deep-down wise people to act in the proper way.

2. As you consider the "listening" proverbs (through 27:5-6), why do you think the writer spends so much time encouraging people to listen to criticism?

3. Proverbs 12:15 describes those who don't listen to advice as fools. Why do people have a hard time taking advice?

4. Since it is so obviously foolish to speak without thinking beforehand (see Proverbs 29:20), why do we find ourselves speaking impulsively?

What are the consequences of responding without reflection?

5. How can we encourage our spouse to listen to us and to reflect on what we say to them?

6. How can we become better listeners?

7. What does Proverbs 13:10 suggest about *why* we don't listen to others, including our spouse?

8. What insights do Proverbs 15:28; 20:18; and 29:20 have for us as husbands and wives who want to improve our communication?

9. Think of some day-to-day practices that can help you establish better habits of listening to your spouse.

▶ **FOR THE COUPLE**

Reflect on how well you listen to each other. Good listening requires these skills and aptitudes:

- Slow to speak—our attention is focused on the other and not on our own words or desires

- Slow to anger—not easily angered, defensive or demanding

- Quick to listen—able to offer back to the other what they've said with accuracy, depth and empathy

- Accuracy—the ability to summarize the content of the communication and link it to other conversations and information

- Depth—what is said is connected to what is known about the person's most significant fears, hurts, dreams and desires—the matters of the heart

- Empathy—willingness to feel in one's body the weight of what you would feel if you were going through the same experience

▶ BONUS

God promised Abraham that he would be the father of a great nation, but the fact that his wife could not get pregnant seemed an insuperable obstacle to the fulfillment of that promise. In Genesis 16 Sarai suggests a way to manufacture an heir utilizing one of the customs of the day, the taking of a secondary wife. Abraham agrees; he impregnates Hagar, and Ishmael is born. In Genesis 17 God reaffirms his promise to Abraham but indicates that Ishmael is not the child who will fulfill that promise. Sarai's advice turned out to be wrong and gave rise to the conflict between the descendants of Isaac, the child of promise, and Ishmael, which has lasted to the present day.

Read Genesis 3:17 and 16:2. What do the stories of Adam and Eve's sin and Sarai's convincing Abraham to take a secondary wife tell us about when not to listen to a spouse?

THE COUPLE THAT PRAYS TOGETHER

"I pray, but not with my wife. I pray for her and for our relationship, but I feel that prayer is a private matter between God and me."

"I feel awkward praying aloud with anyone, even my husband. My words seem clumsy, and I really don't know what to say."

"Praying with my husband makes me feel closer to him. When we share our longings and our hopes and our sorrows and our joys together with God, it's an experience of being bound together in our relationship with the One who is most important."

▶ OPEN

Prayer is the most intimate and powerful form of human communication. In prayer we speak to God. We share with him our most intimate hopes and fears. We praise God for being so great and wise and loving. What role does prayer have in the context of marriage?

▶ DVD REFLECTION

Does the idea of praying together appeal to you, or does it feel uncomfortable? Talk about your experiences with or hesitance about praying together.

▼

CONTEXT: 1 CORINTHIANS 7

Paul is here responding to a group in the Corinthian church that advocated celibacy, even within marriage. He recognizes an important place for those who choose to live a celibate life, but he believes that most people need to get married or else they will be strongly tempted to have sex outside of marriage.

▶ STUDY

With the exception of 1 Corinthians 7, no scriptural text explicitly addresses prayer and marriage. Actually there is nothing like a manual of prayer in the Bible. The second text in this study gives us a broad and beautiful vision of prayer's purpose.

Read 1 Corinthians 7:3-6.

³The husband should fulfill his wife's sexual needs, and the wife should fulfill her husband's needs. ⁴The wife gives authority over her body to her husband, and the husband gives authority over his body to his wife.

⁵Do not deprive each other of sexual relations, unless you both agree to refrain from sexual intimacy for a limited time so you can give yourselves more completely to prayer. Afterward, you should come together again so that Satan won't be able to tempt you because of your lack of self-control. ⁶I say this as a concession, not as a command.

1. What does this passage teach about the importance sexual intimacy has in the marriage relationship?

2. What does your answer to question 1 then tell you about the importance of prayer?

MUTUAL OWNERSHIP

In a culture of radical individuality, we can find 1 Corinthians 7 difficult to appreciate. But Paul expresses a wonderful and important truth about marriage when he says that a husband gives authority over his body to his wife and a wife gives authority over her body to her husband. Of course this is not intended as license to abuse or disregard the body of the other. It is a statement against making one's own desire the sole or prime motivating factor in sexual encounters. I don't own my body; instead I'm called to care for the other. If I don't own my body, I can't require my spouse to serve me, because I don't "own" my desire. Instead I am to care for her body as if it were my own.

Notice that Paul says that in marriage the spouse "gives authority." It is not taken by force, but once that right has been given, it is wrong to withhold sex from one's spouse, except for a season and for the purpose of prayer. We serve each other by an ownership that requires giving primary care to what would please and honor the other. This leads to greater frequency, meaning and joy.

Why does prayer have such importance?

Read Romans 8:22-23, 26-27.

²²For we know that all creation has been groaning as in the pains of childbirth right up to the present time. ²³And we believers also groan, even though we have the Holy Spirit within us as a fore-taste of future glory, for we long for our bodies to be released from sin and suffering.

²⁶And the Holy Spirit helps us in our weakness. For example, we don't know what God wants us to pray for. But the Holy Spirit prays for us with groanings that cannot be expressed in words. ²⁷And the Father who knows all hearts knows what the Spirit is saying, for the Spirit pleads for us believers in harmony with God's own will.

3. Romans 8 tells us that we don't even know what to pray for or how should we pray. As you think about your marriage, do you struggle to know what to pray for or how to pray?

4. Romans 8 seems to major on prayer in times of difficulty and confusion, and sometimes we treat prayer as though it is just

for asking God to help in trouble. What other aspects of prayer are important?

5. Should a husband and a wife spend regular time in prayer together?

Isn't prayer a private matter between a person and God?

6. What can be difficult about praying together as a married couple?

7. How can praying together bless a marriage?

▶ FOR THE COUPLE

We have seen how Paul has linked our prayer and sex life in 1 Corinthians 7. Now take time to evaluate your prayer and sex life together.

What kinds of matters do you pray about?

Does one person regularly initiate prayer? Sex? What does this tell you about what you value?

When do you pray? What posture do you take? Like sexual play, prayer is meant to vary in form, tone, place and expression.

How do you celebrate in sex and prayer?

▶ BONUS

Figure out a reasonable schedule for regular prayer together. Then start doing it!

LEADER'S NOTES

My grace is sufficient for you.

2 CORINTHIANS 12:9 NIV

Leading a Bible discussion can be an enjoyable and rewarding experience. But it can also be *scary*—especially if you've never done it before. If this is your feeling, you're in good company. When God asked Moses to lead the Israelites out of Egypt, he replied, "O Lord, please send someone else to do it" (Ex 4:13 NIV). It was the same with Solomon, Jeremiah and Timothy, but God helped these people in spite of their weaknesses, and he will help you as well.

You don't need to be an expert on the Bible or a trained teacher to lead a Bible discussion. The idea behind these inductive studies is that the leader guides group members to discover for themselves what the Bible has to say. This method of learning will allow group members to remember much more of what is said than a lecture would.

These studies are designed to be led easily. As a matter of fact, the flow of questions through the passage from observation to interpretation to application is so natural that you may feel that the studies lead themselves. This study guide is also flexible. You can use it with a variety of groups—student, professional, neighborhood or church groups. Each study takes forty-five to sixty minutes in a group setting.

There are some important facts to know about group dynamics and encouraging discussion. The suggestions listed below should enable you to effectively and enjoyably fulfill your role as leader.

PREPARING FOR THE STUDY

1. Ask God to help you understand and apply the passage in your own life. Unless this happens, you will not be prepared to lead others. Pray too for the various members of the group. Ask God to open your hearts to the message of his Word and motivate you to action.

2. Read the introduction to the entire guide to get an overview of the entire book and the issues which will be explored.

3. As you begin each study, read and reread the assigned Bible passage to familiarize yourself with it.

4. This study guide is based on the New Living Translation of the Bible. It will help you and the group if you use this translation as the basis for your study and discussion.

5. Carefully work through each question in the study. Spend time in meditation and reflection as you consider how to respond.

6. Write your thoughts and responses in the space provided in the study guide. This will help you to express your understanding of the passage clearly.

7. It might help to have a Bible dictionary handy. Use it to look up any unfamiliar words, names or places. (For additional help on how to study a passage, see chapter five of *How to Lead a LifeGuide Bible Study*, InterVarsity Press.)

8. Consider how you can apply the Scripture to your life. Remember that the group will follow your lead in responding to the studies. They will not go any deeper than you do.

9. Once you have finished your own study of the passage, familiarize yourself with the leader's notes for the study you are leading. These are designed to help you in several ways. First, they tell you the purpose the study guide author had in mind when writing the study. Take time to think through how the study questions work together to accomplish that purpose. Second, the notes provide you with additional background information or suggestions on group dynamics for various questions. This information can be useful when people have difficulty understanding or answering a question. Third, the leader's notes can alert you to potential problems you may encounter during the study.

10. If you wish to remind yourself of anything mentioned in the leader's notes, make a note to yourself below that question in the study.

LEADING THE STUDY

1. Begin the study on time. Open with prayer, asking God to help the group to understand and apply the passage.

2. Be sure that everyone in your group has a study guide. Encourage the group to prepare beforehand for each discussion by reading the introduction to the guide and by working through the questions in the study.

3. At the beginning of your first time together, explain that these studies are meant to be discussions, not lectures. Encourage the members of the group to participate. However, do not put pressure on those who may be hesitant to speak during the first few sessions. You may want to suggest the following guidelines to your group.

- Stick to the topic being discussed.

- Your responses should be based on the verses that are the focus of the discussion and not on outside authorities such as commentaries or speakers.

- Anything said in the group is considered confidential and will not be discussed outside the group unless specific permission is given to do so.

- Listen attentively to each other and provide time for each person present to talk.

- Pray for each other.

4. Play the DVD clip from the *Intimate Marriage DVD* and use the DVD reflection question to kick off group discussion. You can move directly from there to the beginning of the study section. Or, if you wish, you can also have a group member read the introduction aloud and then you can discuss the question in the "Open" section. If you do not have the DVD, then be sure to kick off the discussion with the question in the "Open" section.

The "Open" question and the DVD clip are meant to be used before the passage is read. They introduce the theme of the study and encourage members to begin to open up. Encourage as many members as possible to participate, and be ready to get the discussion going with your own response.

This section is designed to reveal where your thoughts or feelings need to be transformed by Scripture. That is why it is especially important not to read the passage before the discussion question is asked. The passage will tend to color the honest reactions people would otherwise give because they are, of course, supposed to think the way the Bible does.

5. Have a group member (or members if the passage is long) read aloud the passage to be studied. Then give people several minutes to read the passage again silently so that they can take it all in.

6. Question 1 will generally be an overview question designed to briefly survey the passage. Encourage the group to look at the whole passage, but try to avoid getting sidetracked by questions or issues that will be addressed later in the study.

7. As you ask the questions, keep in mind that they are designed to be used just as they are written. You may simply read them aloud. Or you may prefer to express them in your own words.

There may be times when it is appropriate to deviate from the study guide. For example, a question may have already been answered. If so, move on to the next question. Or someone may raise an important question not covered in the guide. Take time to discuss it, but try to keep the group from going off on tangents.

8. The sidebars contain further background information on the texts in the study. If they are relevant to the course of your dis-

cussion, you may want to read them aloud. However, to keep the discussion moving, you may want to omit them and allow group members to read them on their own.

9. Avoid answering your own questions. If necessary, repeat or rephrase them until they are clearly understood. Or point out something you read in the leader's notes to clarify the context or meaning. An eager group quickly becomes passive and silent if they think the leader will do most of the talking.

10. Don't be afraid of silence. People may need time to think about the question before formulating their answers.

11. Don't be content with just one answer. Ask, "What do the rest of you think?" or "Anything else?" until several people have given answers to the question.

12. Acknowledge all contributions. Try to be affirming whenever possible. Never reject an answer. If it is clearly off-base, ask, "Which verse led you to that conclusion?" or again, "What do the rest of you think?"

13. Don't expect every answer to be addressed to you, even though this will probably happen at first. As group members become more at ease, they will begin to truly interact with each other. This is one sign of healthy discussion.

14. Don't be afraid of controversy. It can be very stimulating. If you don't resolve an issue completely, don't be frustrated. Move on and keep it in mind for later. A subsequent study may solve the problem.

15. Periodically summarize what the group has said about the

passage. This helps to draw together the various ideas mentioned and gives continuity to the study. But don't preach.

16. At the end of the Bible discussion, give couples an opportunity to discuss the "For the Couple" section and make the application personal. It's important to include this in your group time so that couples don't neglect discussing this material. Of course, sometimes couples may need to discuss the topic long beyond the five minutes of group time allotted, but you can help them get started in the meeting.

17. Encourage group members to work on the "Bonus" section between meetings as a couple or on their own. Give an opportunity during the session for people to talk about what they are learning.

18. End on time.

Many more suggestions and helps on leading a couples group are found in the *Intimate Marriage Leader's Guide*.

COMPONENTS OF SMALL GROUPS

A healthy small group should do more than study the Bible. There are four components to consider as you structure your time together.

Nurture. Small groups help us to grow in our knowledge and love of God. Bible study is the key to making this happen and is the foundation of your small group.

Community. Small groups are a great place to develop deep friendships with other Christians. Allow time for informal interaction before and after each study. Plan activities and games that will help you get to know each other. Spend time having fun together—going on a picnic or cooking dinner together.

Worship and prayer. Your study will be enhanced by spending time praising God together in prayer or song. Pray for each other's needs—and keep track of how God is answering prayer in your group. Ask God to help you to apply what you are learning in your study.

Outreach. Reaching out to others can be a practical way of applying what you are learning, and it will keep your group from becoming self-focused. Host a series of evangelistic discussions for your friends or neighbors. Clean up the yard of an elderly friend. Serve at a soup kitchen together, or spend a day working on a Habitat house.

Many more suggestions and helps in each of these areas are found in *Small Group Idea Book.* Information on building a small group can be found in *The Big Book on Small Groups* (both from InterVarsity Press). Reading through one of these books would be worth your time.

STUDY NOTES

Study 1. The Power of Words. Genesis 1:1-8; selections from Proverbs.

Purpose: To understand the power of words to create, build up or destroy relationships.

Question 1. Genesis 1 pictures God bringing all of the cosmos into existence by the power of his spoken word. He speaks and it is done. Thus were born the land, seas, stars, sun, moon, fish, birds, animals and human beings. The divine word has the power to create.

Question 3. At first we might think the power of divine speech has no bearing on human speech. However, since human beings were created in God's image, there are analogies between God and us. Certainly we cannot bring things into existence out of nothing, but we can create with our words. Think of Adam's naming of the animals in Genesis 2:18-20. Adam did not create the animals, but under divine guidance, he created the categories by which humans could comprehend the animals.

Human words do have power. A marriage comes into existence when the presiding minister says, "I now pronounce you man and wife." Words can also destroy. This morning the news reported the story of a young woman who testified that her nearly life-ending anorexia was prompted by a single sentence of her high school basketball coach: "You're too heavy; lose ten pounds."

Question 4. Words reflect the heart. A wise person will speak wise words, a fool will utter foolish words. Words are a window into a person's character.

Question 5. Words may dissimulate, but only temporarily. A glaze may cover the defects of a clay pot, but if you look closely you can still see the defects. These proverbs warn people to penetrate beneath the surface of words.

Question 6. The words of the wise lead to safety, honor and life, while the words of foolish people lead to shame, danger and death. According to Proverbs, wise and foolish words have crucial importance to the individual.

Question 7. If words are powerful, reflecting the heart and determining one's fate, then of course the quality of communication between a husband and wife is of utmost importance for the health of their relationship. The unfortunate truth, however, is that we rarely reflect on our speech. We talk impulsively and listen sporadically. The studies in this guide will encourage deeper consideration of how communication shapes our marital relationships and invite thought on how our conversation might improve.

Study 2. Talk That Hurts Relationships. Selections from Proverbs.

Purpose: To understand in order to avoid the foolish talk that damages a marriage relationship.

Question 1. Foolish words are deceptive (10:6; 12:6); sometimes such words are outright lies (12:19) and are intended to hurt the other person (10:6). Foolish words are mocking: they throw up a defensive barrier in a relationship by attacking others (22:10; 26:21).

Question 2. It's a matter of timing. When people are down, they may need someone who can spend time understanding and empathizing with their pain, not just throwing positive-sounding slogans at them. It is critical to understand the frame of mind of your spouse as you talk to him or her.

Question 3. It alienates (11:11) and destroys intimate relationship (11:9). Words can injure (12:18; 25:18) and even kill (12:6). Foolish words can also bring shame (18:13) and trouble (18:7) on those who speak them.

Question 4. The communication problems that can plague a husband and wife are often not much different from such problems in other types of relationships, but since marriage is the most intimate and vulnerable of all human relationships, the stakes are higher. Communication involves listening as well as hearing, and the problem may be with an inability to hear or perhaps with misinterpretation of what one's spouse is saying. Contempt, defensiveness, constant negativity, slander and more can undermine talk between spouses.

Question 5. Failing to take time to talk or indulging in foolish communication patterns will alienate a couple more than virtually any other thing.

Question 6. Self-control. The foolish person has none; the wise person, even when feeling angry, knows how to control the expression of anger. Studies three and four will focus on positive patterns of communication.

For the couple. Our lives are busy, and it is not unusual for married couples to see their time to talk disappear under the heavy load of work, children, church commitments and other relationships. The first step to wise, healthy, productive conversation is to make sure there is regular time to talk.

Study 3. Talk That Builds Relationships. Selections from Proverbs.

Purpose: To understand in order to cultivate wise talk that builds up a relationship.

Question 1. Good communication depends on timing as much as content. *When* you say something is as important as *what* you say.

Question 2. This is something that must be learned, and it can be learned only through observing your spouse and taking note of how he or she responds to tones, gestures and content. Spouses can help each other by honestly stating when feelings are hurt or when a comment helps.

Question 3. Pride puts up a wall in communication and keeps the other person's words from penetrating. Pride especially hates criticism, even constructive criticism. Humility in communication is important. If we do not ever listen to criticism, we are doomed to keep repeating the same bad behavior.

Question 4. The default mode of communication is characterized as gentle (15:1, 4) and kind (16:24). How much easier it is to listen to criticism if it is couched in a tone and manner that indicates that the speaker wants to help and not hurt. According to 25:12, helpful criticism must also be valid. While it is impossible to be right all the time, it is important for the speaker to be as certain as can be that a critical comment is necessary and helpful.

Question 5. As the second part of the parallel indicates, kind words are redemptive for the soul and restorative to the body.

Question 6. Kind words can be critical words (25:12). Indeed, kind words may not feel gentle. Proverbs 27:5 suggests that a rebuke can be positive as well, and a rebuke is an out-and-out verbal confrontation of another. Try to give an example of a rebuke that is positive, helpful and kind.

Question 7. Not all talk is what it appears to be. "Kind" words may be biting and intend harm, while hard words may really be helpful. Sometimes a listener must look for the real meaning beneath the surface of the words. In a marriage especially it is important that we speak to each other openly. If a spouse gets the impression that their partner is dissimulating in conversation, then how can trust develop?

Study 4. A Time to Be Quiet and a Time to Speak Up.
Ecclesiastes 3:1-7; selections from Proverbs.

Purpose: To appreciate the importance of speaking at the right time.

Open. Some talk too much and do not leave a single thought unexpressed. Others have a different problem with self-control and words; they keep too much to themselves and don't share their thoughts with those they love.

Question 1. As we have seen in previous studies, words reveal the heart. If we do not speak, we close off our heart to the other. That is why the person who is married to an overly quiet man or woman feels as if they really don't know their spouse.

Question 2. There may be a host of reasons; we will only mention a few. A major culprit is time. Most couples in the twenty-first century are burdened with so many commitments that little time is left for talk. Another reason may be lack of trust. Perhaps a person has felt betrayed in opening up to their spouse, so they have decided to clam up. Such lack of trust can lead to the development of DMZs (see "DMZs" sidebar), topics that couples have implicitly agreed not to talk about.

Question 3. Those who feel there just isn't enough time need to realize that there are few things more important in their life than building a strong relationship with their spouse by talking regularly. Where there is a lack of trust, this needs to be articulated, and then trust needs to be rebuilt. In both instances, it is important to know that change, though possible, may not happen overnight, but a fundamental commitment to change requires vigilance on the part of both husband and wife.

Question 4. In the first place, the Proverbs passages often equate uncontrolled speaking with negative comments, in particular shaming and angry words. Often it is helpful to process one's anger before speaking rather than letting loose with everything that is on one's heart. There is a time for angry speech, but this should be a last resort.

If someone talks too much, they may overload their spouse so it can't all be processed. Important matters get confused with trivia. There is a time for small talk even in a marriage, to be sure, but we must be careful not to lose what is important in all the verbiage. Spouses who find conversation easy need to be sensitive to those who don't, and those who find it difficult need to work hard to engage their spouse.

Question 5. Those who speak too much can often feel overwhelmed by emotions, to the point that they feel they are going to explode if they don't express themselves. On the other hand, for those who are naturally quiet, self-control entails developing the discipline to speak when they feel like clamming up.

Question 6. For one thing, we should learn from our mistakes. When we lose control and either overwhelm or assault our spouse with our words, we will typically learn that such behavior creates more damage. Or, for those who do not speak enough, lack of self-disclosure leads to distance and disengagement in the relationship.

Question 7. Apparently it is a larger problem that creates significant relational damage.

Bonus. While self-control is more than a matter of our speech,

James tells us that it begins with our words. The tongue is like the rudder that controls the direction of a large boat. A lack of self-control can lead to great relational devastation. James points out that our words are a reflection of our heart. A good heart produces relationally edifying words, while a bad heart produces words that destroy.

Study 5. The Art of Listening and Reflection. Selections from Proverbs.

Purpose: Learning how to listen as well as speak in order to enhance a marriage relationship.

Question 1. Proverbs 18:2 defines a fool as someone who wants to do all the talking but no listening or reflecting. Because of this they cannot be persuaded by the person with whom they are supposedly dialoguing. In marriage this would be a person who did not really care about the spouse's feelings or ideas but just wanted his or her own way.

Question 2. Criticism is the most difficult to listen to. It is easy to hear praise or engage in small talk, but to hear honest evaluations of oneself is difficult, and most people would rather avoid it.

Question 3. To hear advice reveals that we don't have all the answers and that makes us insecure. Often we would rather try to hide our incompetence from others. We do so to feel superior to others.

Question 4. We let our emotions get the better of us. We respond in a knee jerk fashion. When we do so, we usually misspeak and create more trouble and confusion.

Question 5. In the first place, we can encourage a reflective and considerate response by the way we give advice to our spouse. If we attack and accuse or show contempt in our advice, then we are more likely to receive a quick defensive response. In the second place, we need to allow time for our advice to sink in. Often we press our spouse for a response before they are ready.

Question 6. First of all we should cultivate proper humility. We don't have all the answers; we do need help, and God has given us our spouse to help us negotiate a difficult, complex world. Second, we need to discipline ourselves to concentrate on what our spouse says and construe what they say in the best possible light, not easily taking offense. Third, we can help our spouse find constructive ways to share advice so we don't receive it as an assault. We can do that in part by showing our own willingness to change our patterns of speech.

Question 7. In a word, pride. Pride puts up a wall between people, and in particular between a husband and a wife. It is important to learn to be vulnerable with one's spouse. In an intimate relationship between two sinners, there are bound to be many occasions when we can offer constructive criticism.

Question 8. These proverbs call for listening to advice but also reflecting on it before responding. Listening involves more than simply hearing words; it requires reflection. Words are often packed with meaning and emotion, and it takes thought to get at what is really being said.

Question 9. Helpful practices might include the following:

- Notice tone of voice to discern whether the subject matter is important.

- Set down your reading or work when your spouse begins to talk.

- Stop yourself from working internally on your response while the other is still speaking.

- Rephrase what the other person said and ask if that's what he or she meant

- Give eye contact.

- When working through a conflict, take turns talking uninterruptedly for five minutes, after which the other person can summarize what she or he heard you say.

Bonus. Note that listening in the Bible often implies not only hearing words and reflecting on them but acting on them (obeying) as well. When Adam listened to his wife and Abraham listened to his, they acted on what she was saying, and this got them into trouble. This reflects their own moral failure. There are times when the proper response to what our spouse is saying is to disagree and persuade him or her to go in a different direction.

Study 6. The Couple That Prays Together.
1 Corinthians 7:3-6; Romans 8:22-23, 26-27.

Purpose: To encourage couples to cultivate a healthy prayer life together as a foundation to their marriage.

Question 1. Sex is a crucial component of the marriage relationship. Husbands and wives should not use sex to reward each other or punish each other by withholding it. Of course, neither should sex become a matter of marital duty. This passage simply teaches that within marriage sex is not a favor to be distributed on a whim. Such a view goes counter to the idea that each individual is master of his or her own body. Part of the commitment of marriage is to see to the sexual satisfaction of one's partner.

Question 2. If prayer is the *only* thing that may disturb the regular rhythm of sexual relations within marriage, prayer is an extremely important matter! In the first place, the passage assumes that prayer is a regular part of the relationship (the spouses refrain from sex in order to "more completely" devote themselves to prayer). In the second place, prayer is the "only exception" to regular sexual relations between husband and wife.

This passage, which is really about marriage and celibacy, does not tell us *why* prayer is important. Participants may be encouraged to answer from their own experience. Prayer is our primary mode of communication with God, and our relationship with God is the most important of our relationships, even surpassing our marriage.

Question 3. Sometimes we do know what to pray for and how to pray. But often we are at a loss. Sometimes we think we know what is best, but then often find out another way is better. In such cases, it is often better to prayerfully put ourselves in God's hands and be open to how he answers our prayers. For instance, we might pray, "Lord, I want to have a stronger, more intimate marriage. I know I often blow it with my attitude, but I can't seem to control myself. Help me, Lord."

Question 4. Prayer isn't just for requesting God to help us in our trouble. We also direct our attention toward him in prayer. Praise also serves the purpose of reorienting our perspective. It takes our attention off of our own problems and reminds us that we are in the hands of our loving, heavenly Father.

Question 5. In many ways prayer *is* a private matter. Jesus often went off to pray in solitude (Mt 14:23; 26:36; Lk 5:16). He taught that our prayers should not be public shows of piety but rather private devotion (Mt 6:5-6). Yet the people of God are to pray corporately. Psalms was the public prayer book of Israel; the psalms were sung primarily in public and corporate worship. And we have seen that 1 Corinthians 7 reveals how God desires married couples to be in prayer, on rare occasions to the point of fasting from sex for a limited time.

Question 7. Just as individuals should turn to God to thank him for all that he does in their life, so should a married couple. A husband and wife will encounter many troubles in a difficult world, and as they face them together they can turn to God as their defender. Married couples should pray together that God will weave their lives together with God as their foundation.

The prayer itself can be a means of that weaving. As spouses gain freedom in praying together, they will likely find that they know each other in new ways. The vision of God expressed in the praise and petition of each can inspire new vision in the other.